分享快乐

Social Emotional and Multicultural Learning |
Non-Fiction Series

Copyright © 2022 by Level Learning, INC. and Washington Yu Ying PCS™
Original and Edited Text Copyright © 2022 by Washington Yu Ying PCS™

All rights reserved. No part of this book in whole or part may be reproduced without written permission from the publisher.

Published by Level Learning, INC.
Content Contributors:
Washington Yu Ying PCS™
Level Learning - Ya-Ching Chang

Illustrations by: Josh Taira

Leveling classification based on Level Learning standard. For full description, visit www.levellearning.com

ISBN 978-1-64040-081-8
Simplified Chinese Edition

About Level Learning:
Level Learning provides a literacy focused curriculum specifically designed for K-12 Chinese as a Second Language classrooms. Our program offers 20 levels of specific and detailed objectives, leveled texts and passages, mastery-based online assessment, and analytics to enable data-driven instruction. Level Learning reading curriculum for both literature and informational text emphasize grammar and comprehension skills to help teachers develop confident and independent Chinese language readers. The non-fiction series of books are specifically designed to support our informational text course based on multiple national standards. To learn more about our entire offering, visit www.levellearning.com.

About Washington Yu Ying PCS™:
Washington Yu Ying PCS is a Mandarin English dual language immersion International Baccalaureate (IB) World school. Yu Ying's mission is to inspire and prepare young people to create a better world by challenging them to reach their full potential in a nurturing Chinese/English educational environment. Yu Ying's comprehensive IB, dual immersion curriculum equips students with global competencies for success in the real world. As a leader in immersion education, Yu Ying is determined to advance Chinese language programs and global citizenry education by helping other schools create and strengthen their Chinese programs. For more information, email: products@washingtonyuying.org

圣诞节是一个充满快乐的节日。在圣诞节假期，人们会和家人、朋友一起分享快乐。

在圣诞节假期，大多数人会买礼物送给家人和朋友。但是，有一小部分人没有钱买礼物，也有人收不到礼物。

在圣诞节假期，人们会和家人一起庆祝。人们会吃烤火鸡和土豆泥。可是，还会有些人不能和家人在一起，也有些人吃不到烤火鸡和土豆泥。

我们除了可以和家人、朋友分享快乐,我们还可以用其他方式分享快乐。

我们可以去**孤儿院**把礼物送给孩子。和孩子们一起唱唱歌，他们就会很快乐。

我们可以去养老院探望老人。和他们说说话，他们就会很快乐。

我们还可以去帮助那些贫困家庭，送给他们一些需要的东西，他们也会很快乐。

分享快乐很简单。分享快乐不需要很多钱,也不需要很多时间。

一点小小的心意,就会带给他人快乐。你愿意和大家分享快乐吗?

Glossary

	Pinyin	English Definition
圣诞节	shèng dàn jié	Christmas
充满	chōng mǎn	full of
快乐	kuài lè	happy
节日	jié rì	festival
假期	jià qī	vacation
会	huì	will
分享	fēn xiǎng	to share
大多数	dà duō shù	majority
买	mǎi	to buy
礼物	lǐ wù	gifts
送	sòng	to give
没有	méi yǒu	to not have
钱	qián	money
收	shōu	to receive
庆祝	qìng zhù	to celebrate

	Pinyin	English Definition
烤	kǎo	to roast, to bake
火鸡	huǒ jī	turkey
土豆泥	tǔ dòu ní	mashed potato
孤儿院	gū ér yuàn	orphanage
养老院	yǎng lǎo yuàn	nursing home
探望	tàn wàng	to visit
老人	lǎo rén	the elderly
贫困	pín kùn	poor
需要	xū yào	to need
简单	jiǎn dān	simple
心意	xīn yì	kind intention
愿意	yuàn yì	willig

www.ingramcontent.com/pod-product-compliance
Lightning Source LLC
Chambersburg PA
CBHW041222070526
44584CB00001B/52